Love Hard Live Free: Conversations with She

By Shaunteka LaTrese Curry

Poetic Collective Press
Birmingham, Alabama

Printed in the United States of America

Third Edition

ISBN 978-0615459721

Library of Congress Number
 2008920105

Cover design: Mind Spray and Greg C. Graphics

Acknowledgements

To the My Lord and Savior, Jesus Christ, thank you for
being the energy that flows from within to the out.

I would like to thank the one and only Akil Malik Curry for
being my inspiration. Dreams come alive because we stay
inside them.

I would like to thank my Family for being my reflection.

To my Peers
Walk in Love, Speak in light, See in Color

This book is dedicated to the Dreamers

CONTENTS

The Room Collection

Introduction

Love Hard Live Free: Conversations with She is a spiritual triumph. From beginning to end, each poem is overcoming a struggle, a failure, heartbreak, and a let-down. By using me as an example for everything I do, putting this compilation together was a challenge. A challenge not because of the personal affect, but a challenge to make sure each poem grabbed your soul with the intent of releasing only once the book was finished. My thoughts are intended to inspire, heal, and strengthen souls that seek refuge from environments that are tainted with bias.

It is my hope that some word or phrase touches your heart motivating you to want a better understanding of the message.

Every writer knows it's not the words written but the message conveyed...

Enjoy this reflection mirrored on a glass.

Shaunteka LaTrese

RESURRECTION

Venerating this gift, I lift my light towards
you and ask the few to revere me too.
I've come to the conclusion
That consciousness is accountability;
Being the basis of your Inner, seeing the
creative human beings that
Centered into spheres, twisting backwards
Towards the mirror.
Seriously, to have a dream that seems like
a dream yet be the fiend reality
Seen in a dream. You clean?
Released from gravity, I see something
Has to be affecting you about this
situation.
The images are being seen around
unclean, unsanitary, and un-holy being
next to God is cleanliness.
I'm guessing since you don't see me
everyday
It doesn't really affect you.
But, since I'm here in your face about to
Taste the savor of your solz grace
I'm here in the midst of this beast poetic
Speaks tsunami begging for you to
embrace me
 Know that I am mercy on top of humility
that survives she,
I'm here!
I've been here, you just haven't really
Taken a look before
I'm the Tom, the one your Uncle Sam
attempted to
Molest out History

Making my achievements disappear in
books
Books you've made mockery of by
exploiting the things I don't need
Into the things I see daily
Books used to persuade you
Into thinking your Ivy League
Building was put in place
By your educated fathers back
Or this nice manicured land you
Dwell in belongs only to you
Books, Books sometimes lie.
Telling me if I help you (with your evil to
overcome your passé belief
That you run this world) I would be un-
loyal to my family
The same books you used to create plans
and projects
The same projects placed around the
corner from my house
Having me to block out the
Idea of middle class property value
Issuing classifications that all members of
society are subject to the organized public
assistance
Oblivious to the fact that they're dieing,
barely surviving
The spirit of laziness and poverty
Harnessing the wicked ways of the evil
Dutifully lending handouts
Malcolm, Martin and Kennedy
Fought bouts to death, educating those
that lack foundations spiritually.
The political masturbation is that poverty
is a sin! GET OUT!

No plan to get out of this South End.
Wind filled with solutions that this is for
your own good
Seems more abrasive than the north end
that's hiding
Dicks strings in front of the Bush's
Can't blame me right for being curious to
see what the
Collective is going to do in the tail end of
the wrath
I'm here, standing face to face with this
Political Government
You've picked to represent your faith
I'm here, in what's left of the generation
with no cause
But waiting for battle
Requesting the souls with confusion
Seek first
Accustom to begging we're seeking charity
from a foundation we created
Not seeing lies that Congress is reliable
and the movement
That put those in their place can put you
in yours
He states "I have been young now am ole
yet, have I not seen the righteous forsaken
nor his seed beg for bread"
It's in your head
This Movement that must spread
Its personal Dread head,
Picked out afros dead, pseudo naturals
I said!
I'm here demanding respect
That my people are human and
Are subjects to the Systematical

Corporation America
I'm here wakin the dreamers
Spirits deemed as Artist
Soul talkers
Word stalkers
Night walkers
I'm here.

Your Song

There is a problem amongst
The people that the creator
Has chosen as soldiers
The problem is that no one
Knows what to tell and
What not to tell.
I'm told often, you share too
Much, no one wants to know
Your business.
 However, they're appreciative because
What I tell no one knows,
It wouldn't be considered
Personal now would it.
We as humans need to
Learn to keep what's
Meant for us to
Ourselves and keep
What's told by others
Between you and them.
Should we be sharing our
Thoughts with unmeant parties?
I don't think it was meant for
Us to share our thoughts,
The enemy has eyes everywhere
You never know when you may
Be telling your blessings to
Enemy ears
Do you think the creator wants
You to share the thoughts given,
With someone other than the one
It is meant for?
Do you know why it is better to

Speak truth above anything else
I mean to see a past over lap
With what's the future, is just as
Depressing as your present no
Different than what is known
As the past. We caught up!
In the moment, betraying ourselves
You feel like sharing not knowing
That it's tearing your insides into
Who knew that it's all one?
The Mind, the Body, and Soul
It's cold to be so fore right with
What is meant and not
But to speak thoughts into the
Air of an unmeant party could
Cause a ripple targeted at your
Time we should pick and
Choose our friends wise.

BRAVERY

I am not doing what I want to do
but I am doing something
In relation to overcoming the fear of the
Goddess power
Flowing from within to the out
Meeting your danger with sheer valor
I am watching notes carry
Themselves in the air, searching for
chords to fit the vocals.
I hear noise being played statically from
the mistuned purpose
Your instrument is the guided weapon
warrior
Pick up your ears and cry!
I Don't Know Anything About Bravery.
The soul is being grabbed by unfocused
visions
Carrying past transgressions appearing
between the clouds
I'm being touched, ABC's, 123's
I'm being touched, mentally feeling portals
I'm being touched by fears, treachery from
peers.
Tasting the tainted brew beasts preparing
to execute
Disparities against the lost Tribe of the
Diaspora
I and I says, speak to those dry bones
Jiggling inside a spiritual rights struggle
against Governmental
Power and God's Womb.
 Traditional genocide

Being passed down assuming things will change when
Spirituality has been estranged from reality's perception to be, who we are!
KING'S!
I DON'T KNOW ANYTHING ABOUT BRAVERY!
I am the product of a state
That considers hate a social line.
Being blind to Pre-educated white boys burning down churches,
Black boys defending themselves against bully's becoming murders,
Black girls accepting the fact that we're being called the hip hop term of endearment a frank expression of love!
No, it's hate!
You call me anything other than what the creator has named me
I'm slapping ya, not with hands I banded that years ago
My beat down comes verbally
Bringing mental bouts your physical will never come out
I Don't Know Anything About Bravery!
I am the daughter of a seamstress, the daughter of a plant worker by day,
Life hustler by night.
I was born fourth of five, I've survived birf curses,
Traditional worshipping of skin color, hair grades
I've dealt with abuse domestically grabbing me sexually,

Mentally my destiny a played recording
saved
"It's not where you begin but where you
end"
You'll never be anything until you believe!
Knowing the end is always the beginning
Bravery becomes an expression of my
frustration.
 I take my anger and put it into a box sit
inside it and allow God to talk to the paper
Nature request we rest in the
Arms of Birf because we're EARTH!
 WHO TOLD YOU I DON'T KNOW
ANYTHING ABOUT BRAVERY!!

IN THIS HOUSE

Its here...in this house
I watched my innocence raped of the true
meaning of childhood adolescence
Where my cherry was popped by the
Negative perception of being safe.
It's here, in this house,
I stood weak, watching a fragile little girl
Salvage scraps life left on the ground by
her past.
Pieces' being picked from 50 feet back,
Reality slaps 9 into 12
Hell swells the heads of the unspoken
vocals
Its here, in this house,
I see spirits lurking, smirking because the
enemy's plot is being raised and
heightened like the ladder that's broken
Partly appending the transitioning of my
right now from the back when.
Within the mental of the elders,
Flashbacks are hacking the physicals
Like Wall Street stock markets are
hacking the price of natural fruits
For this is something never spoken before
the lower tones of the lone hearted
Mildly setting trends like ill smarted
Its here, in this house,
I needed to be protected like alter boys in
churches. Political asylum being douched
with perverted hands saying those with
sins cast the first stone.
I cast this stone verbally across your tomb

Soon the wicked will be judged just as
they have judged me
See its here in this house I was told that
the disadvantages
Would one day be an advantage?
Smiling you lead me aloof, saying its okay
you'll get over it, under it is more like it
Its here, I watch writings of molestation off
as their only exploring, imploring the acts
performed by an adult to them,
That same adult who never loved himself
because the uncle
That done it to him never loved himself
Its here, in this house,
Where my life got turned around
I was right to run...I was right to fight the
traditional curses passed down making
my ability to choose intention unfound
I was right to renounce physical amenities
inherited for
Its here, in this house, I learned the
meaning of burdens lay
Its here, in this house
I learned the true meaning of agape
Love is not doing something you don't
want to do.
For, love does not know which one to
choose because, love is not a choice.
 It's a rite!
Its here, in this house, hindsight becomes
THIRD knowing here I should have been
The safest, but I wasn't
For it is here, in this house my life met
Purpose

Me, My Soul, She
(Self Sabotage)
If she says write, my pen moves across the
bareness of the page
The stage is set so I press myself into the
center to establish the blessing of it all
If she says sing, my vocals floats pass the
gloom scene that has
Assumed the mind state of fiends, stalled
by the energy she sang,
Bring me your soul
My soul she stole with an attempt to
gather the thoughts quiet kept
Slept on the hard floor blocking the door
because I dreamt she captured me
Sees my eyes as the portal to the abyss
Be's the weakness in my knees as it began
the number 3 list
We's be the foundation of it all yet
We all sprawled across this way, back
your way, up-pass his way
Down her way, they say a mess!
If she says dress, my soul strolls
past the grove
With the armor of a solider
I'm a stand alone my days become long
Building a strong mental
She says be simple, I guess
She says be simple, A mess
She say be simple because
That's the way you're meant to be
perceived
Believed that myself for a second
Still hadn't learned my lesson
I control nothing I am just a vessel

Offering suggestions, lessons
None of the above
I'm just sharing parts of me
The parts of me the sea hasn't drowned
The parts of me the hollow echo
Sounds the ground shakes, I've replaced
the snakes
She says you're not easily approached
Should I be?
Rodents weren't the ones given
The ability to roam free
Is SHE your enemy?

B.C.B.G. Part II
   Be Careful Black Girls

You're joking right!?

Your world is filled with illusions about
conclusions unexplained
You blame your insecurities on the rumors
The mirage has your sight cloudy
Rowdy you seem to want to be,
But that element has never been apart of
me
Publicly, you show a multitude of fake love
behind the doors swirls of
Energy negatively surrounds you.
Be Careful Black Girls
Move your position to avoid the emotion of
regret that begets your generation
Relations are strained to brain point away
from unity
Close to buffoonery
Black Girls, share you with the world.
Stop showing fellas love that you don't
show yourself
I mean, he's aware you have securities
inward stability
Being feed with a spoon
So that gives you mental leeway to commit
to suicide
From being left on the side
Standing watching other brides
Cuz we got to much Damn Pride!
We are guided by a better God
Whose heart is wore across my lust for the
sands to be whole

The goal is to be together
They never explained the classroom
separation would affect
The way we display our love
 It hurts to know we are more divided back
slided into the I-have
Arrived sides of better or lesser
Desperate to be a part of something
Anything was not part of my breeding
I must have slept thru
That end of the brainwash course
Be Careful! With the spirits you allow into
your cipher
The enemy might just suggest you be
something other than the U,
The me, I don't roll wif thicke cliques,
Details about my life is the foundation
To every poem I spit. You'll just have to
take the initiative to locate the
Blind signs between the lines
Allowing this homegrown song to
Be transported from this microphone to
your soul....

            BE BOLD BLACK GIRLS

Right Now: Ode to a Man

The state of being me has me drifting away
from the old she
Used to be the Life of the party, drunk
hardly but elevated
Mentals with a gift you offering a smoke
Choked but the gust remove the feet and
took another seat
Sweet had me weak looking crazy!
Crazy, they called me, Stalled me often
until the real-lies removed the flies
buttered suited in thick Lies
Behind the vibe, cheap!
Think back to the fact of, Hey!
Could this be the real me in love with the
drug no one talks about
The "D"? Dictation being shook giving eyes
a second look
Took me twenty- five to get it, three years
to apply it,
Two years to divine it
Now, I'm here 3 decades into the caves of
the slave mentals
Physical simples and the spiritual aloof
This is proof that the spoof down the
street was not insane
But sane got the brain saying crazy things
Remembering that she's still a child
growing
Showing her seed he can be breeded into
anything he
Chooses to be

See he's lifted, the same as blessed his
choice is anything relevant nothing less
Guess I'm over confident
Graced by evident that He's iridescent,
he's patience, he is a dreamer, he's love
He's humor, and he is humility
He's God; My God bottled down in the
9 year old who has the soul of a man
doing freelance in the Harlem Renaissance
He's a lunch date, the mate that waits
always
Right Now
I see he in me, she in he and we
Are still growing together
That's the goal
To sew positives into negatives, negatives
into compromise
Compromise is when the beehives
Are no longer diluted, polluted with
unthoughtful intentions,
The mentions of remember when's.
What?
Remember he teaches me about the
dreams I once seeded
He sees the she that's fearless
No stress from the he say, she say's
I think they getting it now
My smile is rooted in the
Knowing that I have a great child
 He Smiles because he knows he is
RIGHT NOW!

Grounded

She walked a life talked
About in strife
Gathered key talks to scatter
The hope sought after with age
Notes engaged in a search
The journey, she found that
She the "I" all wrote
Negativity in the open energy
She figured
So she remained introvert
To realize the experts would only
Copy the remnants of the inner
Older, she see's the "we" remaining the
same
Only pretending to jump off the ledge
Said, "It was to be expected."
Since, she has felt the wrath of everything
standing
She sees the past as foundation
To last solid having a personal relation
with the maker, the fakers become
breakers only wanting to hate,
They can't.
I'm made out of respect
Demanding you have nothing
But what you choose to see
She is me
Knowing that nothing less than humbled
blessings be placed on your path
The creator has placed you
In the center of favor and grace
Mercy was the calmest of states
comforting at the right times

Seemed almost too needy
Wanting all or nothing
Explaining to submit or nothing will be
offered

I RISE

Born blind from the dark
I entered the smog with two eyes bleeding
From reality slapping me I felt a cold hand
The same hand has been on my bottom
Saying, Society is not the problem
Society is not the problem?!
You're only saying that so I won't invoke
The skeptism molding my soul to
Revolt...rebel...Get free
Born blind, I find that nothing is by
chance
Destiny only enhances the probability of
dreams
Themes that brings the light into dark
Sparking Déjà vu of pasts lives
Souls cry from that cold hand on my
bottom
Saying, "Society is not the problem"
No, it's not!
We are the cause of the unresolved
equation. I'm talking to the daises,
The ladies, the Queens sent to lead breed
Kings by positive means,
None demanding beliefs
We happen to be the tea inside the bag
controlling the brew,
Bitter and sweet.
We are so used to the plantation
dilapidation of self
We've decided to settle for what's left.
Falling in suit with the deaf, dumb, and
blind
It's time to share our designed;

To birf nations, dissolve frustrations and
heal the sighted
Born blind she designed us to be the light
without sight
Speaking truth in circles to be proof
That nothing is really aloof
It refuses to be the example of the ability
to see supernaturally the truth
I RISE.

Consider This...

The need to mingle with the sane is
blamed when the insane
Gets respect by staying within the frame of
the concept
We as a race of people should want to go
beyond what we are told,
Search to be whole, and seek to be palms
We dwell on rocks as if they are
mountains,
When mountains have become volcanoes
We are still talking about a war when the
Revolution began years ago
Come on Joe!
Why you acting like you don't know
If you don't, I can tell you how it was
shared to seek out two books
The Koran, the Holy Bible utilize the tools
as proof
 The Comparing of the parable is sharing
the land given
However, we have been living as if we've
earned it when we didn't.
Just sent to prove we were able to blend,
mix, and mate yet, all we're displaying is
death, greed, and hate!
Let's bring you up to speed!
You have to get a little bit of everything to
see the med
I'm here offering a foundation, a start to a
relation
One on one with the maker, it might help
Over stand the spiritual warfare
Placed in the land of men

There is a demand on minds that find
Time to seek, read, learn, live and breathe
Right Knowledge
We have been standing in shadows with
shame, for what?!
Speak out about Social Injustice,
                    Spiritual Poverty,
                    Genocide Harvesting
Like sands we walk with lasting souls,
Demand your Birf Rites
Consider this as insight on
How to get your Third sight on right and
off the hype!

CONSIDER THIS!

TERMS

I'm coming to terms with my over beaten
heart impressed with your soul
I can see how it may seem like I'm not
serious my
Nonchalantness takes control
Within minutes im expecting the
supernatural to
Shock the spirit leaving a print palmed
next to mine
Against the water stained glass
Colors in red, black and green
I've seen it all in a dream but not
everything happens-in the none scripted
see...
I'm coming to terms
With my missing mouf fixtures exposing
my smile DELIGHTED
In the presence of your humbleness
Being down to earth...
I never imagine you were the 9 month
waiting period from the 3 year
conversation series...
I'm thinking you should let go of the
apprehension.
 Physical intentions are showing
Yet, sitting on your left brain is the debate
of whether you should or shouldn't
I'm in a season of life where I am no longer
searching
For that period piece fairytale,
I'm begging for my eyes to swell with
laughter tears

I'm begging for my ears to ring from the
mood swings of us sitting on mental limbs
Begging for the AM's to stay
I'm coming to terms with the ingested
caterpillars
Exposing intuition
My stomachs overwhelmed with the
expectance of a spiritual birf...
You are my earth...
The beginning of my sanity,
The ending of the enemies attack on the
fact that I am a Queen...
I'm coming to terms with my rites being
mother of earth,
In the stars our souls write birf names
Twisted backwards towards the east
Peace you are, full of the creator's energy
I see the seeds lay invoking ancestry in the
West
You are the King that will lead the cruel
hearted to the spiritual means of release.
You are peace!
 The peace that holds the end of realities
deferred in dreams waiting for the opening
scene
I've come to terms!
The aura holding your frame
Is meant for me
Themes releasing the metaphoric
epiphany
Surpassing a childlike reality
Up there our souls dance
Anticipating the never ending dare
That mentally, I beat you

PONDERING: AM

I was wondering if you think about me, as
often as I think about you
I mean, daily I'm restless in your solitude
The condition that has my mood soothe
within the minted peppers of your scent
Transforming the day into different ways
found to express myself
I was wandering if you think about me,
Drifting into your depth exploring the
calmness of your presence
You excite me-into the womb-man birfing
nations of positive teachers and spiritual
healers
Controlling the energies with beats that
makes the heart warm
Love that numbs the tongue
You're capturing my transitions
With the NU
Your demeanor being the reason for my
mood
Are you okay wif being my thought
process?
Would I be wrong to stain you in my
mental frame?
Assuming my heart might not like being
told what to do; I can stop if you like?
I need you to know
I was wondering if you think about me, as
often as I think about you
You're the step I haven't managed yet
The secret I'll not share
You got my mind focused on just being
Divine in your own presence

My fickleness now seems none pessimist
Know on my right side you walk, into my
left ear you whisper
Truths about my gift and lay foundations
to our plantations
I was wondering if you thought about me
Today, yesterday, the day
before.....tomorrow?!
Perhaps, I should hold my breathe
Suspended between the ladex of my
spiritual desires
Knowing the physical is only subliminal
Mentally wanting our souls to combine
I mean, I feel you here
Right here in between the Perception and
the Black Is of the Ground Fertile
Right here in between the She Was and
the Breathe of the Echo Effect
I feel you right here between you are and
obsession
I was wondering, I've been wondering
Now it seems like pondering almost
Do you think about me?
I mean who wouldn't. I am the tree
bridging your trials
Between waters muddied and holy ground
Shoes come off just to greet. I am the
release that has the
Collective spitting flames like beasts
U think about me!
Knowing I am your filter,
Disposing the daily trash like workers of
sanitation except on Mondays
Your heartache becomes peeled layers of
oranges placed in shoots

Revealing the part of the conversation
that's the hardest
I'll talk to later darling... Good Morning!

Is Like

So this is what it's like
Lights are bright vision blurred
From ultra electric shock
A wave of stages inside my brain
Connecting thoughts thru patterns
Of transferred energy
Locks picking the shackles apart
See the richness of unity bring souls
Thru the enemies walk
Perhaps, shock could be my first
Response as my heart swells thru the
Passion pumping purple from
The eye third above the womb chakra
I shocked you didn't
I surprised you with the why not
instead of the why.
It's okay to cry, the expression
Says that you are aware of yourself
And my ability to impact you.
Is what it's like compared to the
Beauty of the waves crashing
Into the sand, passing slowly to
The side revealing white pearls sparkling.
Is what it's like, flashing amorously
In the open field, flowing thru the breeze,
Climbing trees swinging with carefree,
Fearless visions?
Is what it's like the component to
Capture the essence of love
inside a moment?
It's the exceptional, ordinary
Doesn't exist in the this category
I'm a Kingdom child, the Queen standing

On the podium composed of your
Diamond eyes
Your heart filled with gold and
That crystal frame called your back
It's like the moon rose displaying
Shadows of two people standing with
One figure
Revealing the true treasure
Planted in your spirit
This is what it's like!

Apples, Oranges, Grapes

I'm waiting for the one to help pick out
grapes
Dates have placed my vines behind the
expected timeline for harvesting.
Causing me to think thoroughly about the
Choices previously made
Normally, I'll harvest the crops solely and
have control, not knowing I was wrong.
This information wasn't shared with me
I haven't been willing to accept help
But, who needs help picking out grapes?
If that's a task for two, then, I know I was
not the only one aloof to the fact that the
time should be shared.
The grapes not people
So, I wait outside the mistakes previously
made, after the communication was
shared from the local grocery explaining to
me it would be vain to allow just anyone to
pick fruit
When most aren't familiar with the crop
Let alone the seeds they're harvesting
You have got to be jokin
I'm on the verge of being sane and you're
telling me most can't pick fruit because
they lack mental proof?
She nodded saying, "Yes!"
Explaining she dreamed of the proper
feast, her crop wasn't harvesting grapes
"I'm working with something that carried a
little more weight,"
Apples and oranges

Something real easy who wouldn't know
how to pick out oranges and apples that's
something that comes natural
She informed harvesting took one season
"believe me it wasn't as easy because, I
wasn't doing the picking,"
Not to mention my make up is different
I wouldn't want the next to wash my
dishes
So, I listen as this voice told me in the
palm of your hand stands
The base with a soft palate
To represent the bloodline
Holding an apple is natural
So I didn't hesitate to the take the bait
However, you're harvesting something
supernatural controlling the power of
thousand years
A Goddess she is distinguishing the color
base of vines needed to appear dark for
the wine and
Sometimes the harder they appear doesn't
mean it's clear that they are ready to be
plucked.
What is ready to be plucked?
Your destiny!
 To have the smoothest red wine harvest
You'll have to wait for the supernatural
Eye to take the bait

Apples, Oranges, Grapes

OH YEAH!

I'd go ballistic for some hot stuff right now!
How have the things become so corny?
Shortly it seems where the theme's not
money, bootie, she's a lesbian, thespian is
what I meant
Hey you thought he went with the thick
chic?
Who cares, do dares with ya time,
Find that right knowledge and polish it up!
Get off that lazy spirit, do some tricks with
your mind
The divine is calling; sit out if you're not
ready for this bout
Because the revolution is personal
First of all, find focus within
Stop depending on the demand of the bull
Shivers I used to get,
So much is spent on listening
For the wrong no wonder this presence is
so strong
16 bars and a look
What song have you been Humming?
I'm coming out of the city
Longing for something Nu, instead I
drifted into something blue

OH YEAH!!

A Testimony: What is true?

Yes baby, spirits dwell among us as
individuals
Only difference is they're invisible to the
unconscious?
The conscious see the dreams themed
As revelations taken place
Meaning we are aware of what we
Do and put out with No Doubt screaming
"Sunday Morning"
Worship God with speaking truth
Don't façade your intentions with wishful
Dimensions of a third world party
The sky is meek and the distant future
bleak with promises that I never
Feet standing poppy seed eye thought
They were planted solid
Knowledge is my vanity,
Beauty my curse
First recognize that all negativity simply
demise from a plot
That was rehearsed
Just say the days of unneeded, Spoon feed
like an open wound
Spoon feed like a toddler.
Dollar for dollar being sold a
Half told bird
This chic got you up against a wall that's
got you sprawled
From half north way split backward
Don't try to figure the design of the words
Just like birds: We flock
Don't stay in that mind past the
designated date

Or are we monkeys
Can't believe what we sometimes see
The face is always a mirrored me
From the vintage clothes, with an Ole sol
sent to reap on minds
Harvesting a righteous truth
Goddess within the means of Hearing and
seeing,
Walking and talking, Religious and
spiritual
Debating over something you've already
been leaning on!
The journey is but so long
With strong dation found within a country
mile of a smile
God gives each cistern
A physical dressing, two mental
expressions with
Five means of sight
A thousands years ago my craft was
released giving
My sol free peace to time travel
Having nothing more than the next (with
text)
Heated they seemed under covers
After a wet dream
Dippers and dappers, Thieves and
grabbers
All receive the same waves just to a
different bird like
Flying within your mind hiding
We growing, the knowing
Exist of unseen is phenomena
Eye mean to believe in the unseen
Is truth alone?

God is amongst us dwelling as souls
The pins of your knees holding the joints
across
The wrist line being designed with a fine
chemical
The divine is a mind open
With the right knowledge to seek truth
Like birds.... They grew.

I met a woman once
Who considered self to
Be the original of what?
I am not sure.
But, she was that and a lot more
She was thinking, speaking, Acting wrong
and a challenge.
What do we do with challenges?
We wait them out!
I knew what I wanted out of the situation
Knew I wasn't getting what I wanted.
How bout if truth is game.
Why relay the memo by omission to save
face like the casa of novas
Why lie?
I love her though, with every essence of
eucalyptus dripping off my locs
It was sometime like being slowly
electrocuted over and over again while
being in her presence
My roots would begin to entangle as if
their making out.
My skin would be so moist; my body
would ache with fever
I could never find that calm spot while
around
This woman carried energy that has
grabbed my soul and has held on ever
since although, her face is like a memory
to me her spirit forever dwells within
The Queen that centers my being
REALITY!

REMAKE

Give it all you got. Give it all I got.
You've taken to long to claim a spot on
highways
They're called by ways, 4 ways to dreams
sometime
Seems to be unbelieved as real
Oh, but yesterday, I remember you saying
Your life will be like none other
You see most are smothered inside the
perception
Of what the outside feels they should be
When they can't even see
Really, on yesterday, it got quiet enough
for me to
Hear you say, "You are on your way"
Steadfast try not to stray
Stay away from the likeable mic
And that's how you know your right
I've grown into a tree that's
Tall and slender
Brown and tender
Bendable and unbreakable
I have the ability to flow and be blown by
the strongest of winds
Yes, depending on the force of energy
I can even lie down for days only to rise
with the gaze of a prophet's face
Having the ability to weather any storm
Timeless, I'm suppose to be this way
I'm a palm
Remake me

STAY

One day eye want to wake up and
not have to feel the
Reminder of your presence
Nearer that day when eye can speak to
you and not have
Some type of remorse or regret from what
could have been and could come to be
Can you help me see?
The way to the other side where my clouds
are not filled
With a drenched rain from a soul crying
free me, release me, please!
I give up what's the use, do I succumb to
the defeat?
That eye never had a chance or
Do eye look at the real-lies before me and
spitfire like dragons
At my foes that taunt me
My days continue to be a reminder of
something that
I'm just waiting in line for
Right now, I'm in a state
Of being me yet, the glimpse of Ur eyes
Before my lids raise afraids the fear of
achieving a multipurpose goal
Inside my soul is anxious and unwilling to
comprise for that
Has happen
Still there's this unforgiving
Potion flowing like a poured emotion from
Root to end lock
I'm in shock!

How long have I been feeling this way?
Eye find that my thoughts
Stray your way more often than twice,
Nice,
I mean eye thought I'd released
This energy since it was so plainly stated
That we could never be together because
 "I didn't know how to talk to you"
My soul laughed, because it's like a
feather
The situation that is.
Now, my thing,
I'm not sure if you were a slap in the face
or letting me know my place
Did you know you were saying one thing
yet doing another?
Was that feeling there before or after you
smelled my lavender?
I know I can't have everything
My way, but, you could have stated that
from the go
Instead of slow poking my stroll
I'm sorry, I'm coming across rude
I'm a prude with envy for your situation
for the moment
That is a situation I had once
That is still waiting for the reuniting with
a long lost sol
With the time in between I stand at the
edge of the pier watching the tide
Roll pass, with message filled glass rolling
away. Waiting for the moment to comfort
you and allow this day to be finished
Stay!

DA PERFECT PEACE

I had a dream last night
A dream so real I woke up
A dream so real it made me choke
Words stuck inside the cerebral
Portal floating to the box
Hoping vocals pick up
To allow my scream to release
This peace was perfect
Right place,
Right time
Designed to incline
Me and mine, his, yes, His
I see your face every night
As my lids meet
Just as angels grab me
We greet in our special place
No interruptions
You and I sitting in green pastures
Giving mental orgasms
Eating apples, oranges and grapes
The perfect escape
The situation being elevated
With liquid libations
Not red, not grape, but White
Merlot and Chardonnay was
Sprayed to ease the tension
In the moment
This peace is just my relief from
The grief that has been haunting my sleep
The awaken state has me mistaken
For a believer of what's seen
When I was born dwelling in dreams
I was born in your dreams

I came alive the same dream you
First hugged me a physical greeting
Of two souls mating I began waiting
The same dream we had our first date
The acceptance of our soul's destiny
The same dream you proclaimed
God sent you to be my mate
Because I asked him to
So I'm inclined to be the
Walk of your back bone
The stroke of your soul,
Not the ego
My stroll is the representation
Of your God like qualities
Feeding your expected embrace
I'm swayed forth and back
Jazz tune last played
I'm clued,
I'm in tune, I'm in tune
To your being well beyond wise
We are anxious to take our space
So when you look at me
I see the beat of my heart
In your eyes smiling
I realized
I had a dream last night
A dream so real I woke up
A dream so real it made me choke
Words stuck inside the cerebral
Portal floating to the box
Hoping vocals pick up
To allow my scream to release
THIS PERFECT PEACE

Weathered Heat!

It sits on me with harsh humidity
Seeping thru my lower lip
I...took a sip of evaporated water
Slaughtered I'm getting collared
By the white beaten seeing blue
Choked from the smoke you're
Breathing on me
See your fullness of body is fogging sight
No longer can I distinguish day and night
This thing is getting me down
Got me wet from neck frown can't smile
this cloud is blown
The release is seeking the next 144
Swore I'd stay away twice
It'd be nice if your glare wasn't
So bright affecting my sight to
Search for the corrective lens I don't like
So I'm rolling on blind sight and miracle
ear perception
Tripping off societal conception that I can't
take the heat
So I don't cook in the kitchen
Phish phyr's are had on a daily basis but
that I don't care to mention
You've got me thick breathing like wheezy,
What happen to moving on up?
You're angled 90 degrees over
The trees that are 45 paces away
From the cat I've been chasing
About my 10 dollars cause
He only gave me 15 plus a bill
I'm still in this mucky serenity

You're offering as global warming
More like a warning!
You're showing your big, red,
Orange, hazy assuming you care
We didn't take care of our
Environment properly
So you decided to show your
Wrath early surely you can
Understand weak you are not
It's just HOT!
I'd rather weather the heat
From my spot
Inside the window seal

I am somewhere in between
Cyndi Lauper and Bjork none Middle age
mother trying
To have fun enjoying a son that is slowly
Revealing it self
I am always behind because I have been
known to decline
Clique type offers not realizing
I'm softer when seen alone
Alone is what I'm used too.
Getting had me downs No need to offer
frowns
Because these are suppose to be the good
times
So in solitude island back to wait for the
walls to fall
I am somewhere in between
What most have seen yet not quite used
to?
I am somewhere in between what most
want to believe they're
Capable of and their actual deeds
I am in between nowhere and somewhere
However right in the middle
Of nowhere seeing everyone around me go
somewhere other than where they're
Supposed to be going
I am somewhere in between
The suchimuch and ghetto ruts
I am somewhere in between
My dreams and reality seeing
I'd rather be me
Somewhere in between

A Libra: What's really going on!

My mind races fast against the clock of
time
Flying by like 7 years past and my last
time saying
I'll try or I might, but I will be ready and
available for the
Necessary things in my life
Be mindful of how your actions say
I love you
More often than your words
Say thank you when you know deep
In your heart that the outcome could have
been different
But your soul stead fast in the midst of
the storm
The storm being the warm third party
mediator
Between your self and God
How warm is it to know you have the
support of
A family with a home to return to
What is a home?
Some say the home is where the heart is
Then I have a lot homes in a lot of
different places
Because my heart is torn with
So many hurts dividing my insides to its
weakest moment
Thus along my journey
I find strength in knowing there is
A Balance

The Room

This Collection contains poems written in
a period of my life that was very dark. It
would be very easy to say that I
understood the purpose for writing them
at the time but I didn't. Recently, I came
into the understanding that anything that
can cause depression is a cause to
worship.

Shaunteka LaTrese

The Room: A Cup of Tea

Would I just settle in my life?
Have open matters that revealed
A nature never searched or seen
Thoughts about truly I do love you
Eyes shut wide
Feelings my body thought,
Images my mind saw
Committed by pressure
Settling my present...while
Denying my person any refreshing
Simply made soul finding mine
But she wasn't running
Heart of the same mind
She wasn't crying
Expecting more than I wanted to offer
Demanding the given
Wanting what others had,
Having what many wanted
Haunted by envy looming over relations
Jilted by social segregations
A CUP OF TEA

The Room: So

So, Knowledge only can be upset about
something's
Knowledge is upset because you failed to
consult her
You failed to seek
She's been over looked
Doesn't matter if you have great things
outside
Stop fooling yourself and wait your turn!
Season is mine?
Believe or Not 2 MC's can not occupy the
same space
At the same time
Yet must I get in a line
What am I waiting on? Waiting for
G.O.D.O.T.
God of determination over tribulations
May or Not ...you won't wait long
You taking the lines of strong beliefs and
discarding them
Da next week....

The Room: Quarter

Can 25 be divine? If the time to find
yourself
Is 7 times that of 25 minus my time
 Only to know that you've known
What you want and were from the first day
The 13th star aligned with the seventh
moon heaven
Collided from a spool of thread
Was woven into the Queen that centered
by
Being between Mercury and Venus
Allowing the world to seek face in all that
was
Natural
Is that divine?
To foretell a future given six lives ahead
Of mine
I am the furtive, a life done in secret to be
Opened and unveiled
As the life of a quarter
I'm talking Divine Order!

The Room: Peace Break

Set time aside to give peace offerings, to
makers of positive ciphering
Bring elegance to naturals healing minds
spiritually
Giving signs that time has come.
Be peace sistren
Cyphern smiles dials 700 situated miles
Given shouts mind out to butterflies
branded and tan
Naturals transforming minds to divine
Healing makers smiles from frowns
...drowning
In self apathy giving vasectomies
mindlessly to the unneedy
Greedy fools coming cool thru from the
windows breeze
Freeze! Has it set yet? That speck of treach
Still set in our mind state.
Hate! Is a sickness Earthyz path was to
draft
Open minds and warned hearts with locs
4 days and ways to heal the greedy
helping the needy
Find that weather raising tsunamis in my
heart
That's the part we never get
Your mind state is preset!

The Room: Now What!

Response! Simply divine is the statement
of being simple.
Why? Can't there be another vine that
shall be
Entwined in my mind
What if? The statement of being divine is a
relation of ships
Being rocked between you and I
What if? Why, isn't the need now, for I
have tried to quiet
This storm but the peace you speak will
soothe no more
What If? Your response to everything I
spoke wasn't
"Well I don't know what you want me to
say!"
How bout! When spoken words are nicer
and sweeter
Deeper you'll be allowed like a felon in my
mind
To explore wilds
How Bout! At this late date a longing
Is of procrastination for our sols have
already fixed our destination
What if? My molecular sunshine could
only be brought about by you,
What would you do?

My Three Faults

An awakening from me
She saw three of her faults following
For I had been enslaved by brain
To think I wasn't enough
For me had watched friends build ships
And foes meet common goals
All awhile she sat and met every fault
gathered
From past lives
Now 6 lives with a score under a belt of
70lbs
Poured happiness across a heart
Of hurt and war scars
Realizing that every year was for me
Every lie told and heard was for
She
Then I woke up to see she had an even
longer
Journey ahead instead
I wave

The Room: Maintenance

Overwhelmed by outside interference, as
volumes of electricity
Flow thru my vains
Current attractions present local pains.
Controlled by evil intent
 Lustfully, I think of how this night can
result in eventful passion
Or consciousness of two minds elevated.
Won't allow the nemesis to decide these
relations as tainted
Impressive lies and deceitful styled fables
Consummating the relations
Neither I nor she can see
Never-ending tells of how confused I think
I am or want to be
Confused when this lady has presented
Nothing but her love
Not confused when peers displayed intent
to destroy
A bond made unbreakable by our souls
Control has been accessed
Retrieval denied
The mind can not express its most
Intimate and detailed thoughts without
Signs from our times

MAINTANENCE

The Room: Jaded

Now I walk jaded
Jaded line I walked as my mouth could
talk no more
I saw my present pass like 5th period class
Futures on how to portray elegance
granted only from she
Telling others she's not the one for me
For why has this young lady spat dat
mess!
No she is not for me becuz
I am with her the other of my lovers the
one
True fiend of breed, my kind
Did you see?
She peeks at me from the side of eyes like
following wreckers
Carrying worn tires of cars picking glass
From streets of broken jaws has your face
been replaced?
Nope, cracked and on the ground.
Jaded was my line
I was blind Images I thought I saw
confusion
I thought I brought
4 why
Broken patois spoken out the side of her
Jamaican Vibe
Mother Earth you are not
Spitting that about the white mans this
and the "man's" that.
Cute Outfit, is that from the Gap?
That store is not black owned. You're the
Clone!

The Room: Faces

Faces seen though unseen
Thoughts brought to the
High esteem of self
Pictures a fly-buttered black
Through me
You know death is a process of self
Self is a body of High Righteousness
Processed to achieve self esteem
A lover... Walks of all... Life eternal
Storage of souls deteriorate
Coolers being made to participate of
3 scores of 6
Crack open and step out
See the hell
Made for us by us
Be a GOD my brother
Sisters see QUEENS not fiends
Achievers Process the blackness
Lovers of life make truth
I am eternal because I see the
 Blackness in ME

The Room: Eyes Have It (Shaunteka's Eyes)

Eyes green before my person is seen
Girl, don't buy into the prison
That has been created
We are all queens
Moon ¾ of full and breast aren't yours
might
I haven't spoken of any negativity
Surrounding your aura you're not even in
plain sight
Why fill your portal with spite that only
consumes and wounds intelligent to speak
of others with a soft tongue and warm
hearts
You're the one with defaults and battered
charts
See dreams and map plans of rebuilding
A love that will only be shown not told
A love...Preservation of self...Hating
A love of self that is expressed
While the smiles tear frowns, devils drown
Within you... Yes they do
Celebrate the beauty of a lady
See that same smile as you see a love
that's down frowned
It's you working progress
The eyes have it.

The Room: Da Mission

Why be a fool
When you control what's yours
Why be a fool
Soul Patterns creates situations
That you have to resolve
In order to move on
You have the presence
Of a great one
Control only what happens to you
What about things you can't control?
They don't exist
All things are controllable ask GODOT
He'll show you, Accountability
Seek knowledge and wisdom ...it will find
you
Seek power through Daknoc ...you will
know it
Seek Fame and Fortune...you will have it
but,
You will not like it
Do not seek things that can not be
handled
Search for things that are needed
Patience is of virtue on your journey
Da Mission

The Room: Electric Material

Elevated Minds entwined in
A conversation of sex... (Who got next?)
Trying not to flex whose
Necks most powerful...
Shall we drift away?
For a brief stay of free easy thinking?
Can we spray the things?
Thought and felt not saw or heard,
Like birds I fly thru you
For the thought process has been
enlightened,
By the potential of your soul!
Not Gold or Silver.
Will you share your Crystals?
Balls where souls search,
Futures when the present hasn't even past
Have you even seen a looking glass?!
Patterns are reflecting
The presents of potentials
Plants grow from processed Roots...
While connecting souls are being
Processed likes boots
MARCHING in the MIND
Not blinding your mind
With petty thoughts of physical infections
Accepting injections of subliminal
Messages
Maintaining weakness for a sexual
deepness

The Room: Dealings

Dealings are never easy, yet to settle is
To settle for a style
That fades after awhile
To settle for a book that
You haven't even looked
At the bottom of your heart
You feel the start of a wonderful thing
That you find not to be
The mediums of all evil
Spoken from all righteous
Never have I seen you not right us off
So parlay with a stray dog
You picked from the pound of beauty
You never choose or found
To settle for a life that KARMA will fight
To settle for the thoughts
Someone else has bought
To miss guide your passion
To mislead you dreams
Your everyday Dealings
Leads you to the wrong things
Only one suggestion decides your fate
NEVER SETTLE FOR A FALLIN MISTAKE

About the Author

Shaunteka LaTrese, Birmingham, Alabama native currently living in Atlanta, Georgia. She is an artist in every essence of the word. Shaunteka has a classic soul that sings psalms and breathes life into situations grasping for air. Mixing her life experience as an artist, model, and cutting edge fashion sense allows the reader to be captivated with vintage imagery twisted in a modern flash. The Rhythm in her heart beats through each word singing song on paper. Shaunteka empowers the readers to find their inner peace and be accountable for the energy they posses.

www.ingramcontent.com/pod-product-compliance
Lightning Source LLC
Chambersburg PA
CBHW060159070426
42447CB00033B/2223